Bloom & Sip

A Faith-Inspired Guide to Watering Your Spirit

Sorena Washington-Briley

Bloom & Sip: A Faith-Inspired Guide to Watering Your Spirit

Copyright © 2025 by Sorena Washington-Briley

All rights reserved.

Scripture credits:

Unless otherwise noted, Scripture quotations are taken from The Holy Bible, New International Version® (NIV®). Copyright © 1973, 1978, 1984, 2011 by Biblica, Inc.™ Used by permission. All rights reserved worldwide.

Scripture quotations marked KJV are from the King James Version (public domain).

Disclaimer: This book shares personal experience and encouragement. It is not medical, legal, or mental-health advice. Please seek a qualified professional for guidance specific to your situation.

ISBN (paperback): 979-8-9999989-2-7

Cover photo: Sorena A Photography LLC

Cover design: Bloom & Sip Press

First edition

Printed in the United States of America

For permissions or bulk orders: bloomandsipguide@gmail.com

Connect on Instagram: @bloomandsipguide

TABLE OF CONTENTS

Welcome

If you're reading this, you are right on time.

This workbook isn't about perfection or having it all together. It's about watering your spirit, honoring where you've been, and letting new things grow. I've walked through storms, heartbreak, family secrets, and starting over, but every season, yes! even the hard ones, taught me something about blooming.

As you move through these pages, know this:

- » You are worthy of healing.
- » You are allowed to start again.
- » You can bloom, right where you are.

Think of each page like a sip of something warm, meant to restore, not rush you.

Let's sip, reflect, and grow together.

With love,

Sorena

Start Here

Take a deep breath and settle in.

This workbook is your safe soil, a gentle space to tend to your spirit, water your dreams, and make room for new growth. Some pages might feel easy, some might challenge you, and others might meet you exactly where you are.

Just like a garden, your spirit needs care, water, sunlight, and time. There are seasons of drought and seasons of rain, times of pruning and times to flourish. Every season counts. Every part is sacred.

Give yourself permission to go at your own pace. Some days, you may want to write a lot. Other days, you may just need to sit quietly and let a sentence or a prayer soak in. There is no "right way" to heal, to reflect, or to grow.

Let this be your invitation to listen deeply to your own needs, to honor your progress, and to notice even the smallest signs of blooming.

How to Use This Workbook

Keep a pen and a notebook nearby so you can jot down your reflections, scriptures, prayers, or any breakthroughs as they come to you. Sometimes the act of writing helps you see things more clearly and remember them later.

» **Read** each chapter as a conversation, let the story and guidance settle in.

» **Reflect** honestly; don't edit yourself. This is your space to be real.

» **Practice** the exercises and try new habits as you're ready.

» **Return** to the parts that water you most. Growth is a cycle, not a straight line.

Let's begin.

Chapter 1:
Rooted in God's Presence (Put God First)

Some mornings, the world feels heavy before you even open your eyes. Maybe you wake up to noise, worries, a to-do list running wild in your head, or memories that still sting. On days like that, what do you reach for first? I used to reach for my phone or just lay there, hoping the day would magically feel lighter.

But I grew up with a different kind of start. My mom, wise, devoted, and loving, believed the best way to begin the day was by honoring God first. She'd press her Bible into my hands before school, ask me to read Psalm 23 out loud, and smile as if she knew some secret. I didn't always appreciate it at the time, but now I get it: she was giving me armor. She knew the world could be unkind, but she also knew God would meet me wherever I was. So even after I had Psalm 23 memorized, she had me still hold the Bible in my hands and speak the words out loud, because to her, that made it living and real. As I got older, I found my own ways to put God first. Sometimes it's gospel music in the background as I get dressed, letting the words soak into the walls and my spirit. Sometimes it's just a quiet prayer, thank you for waking me up, help me walk with purpose today. How I open my day changes, but the reason stays the same: I choose to give my first thoughts and energy to God.

You don't have to do what I do. You don't have to be perfect, or spiritual. Putting God first is personal. It's a decision. It could be a prayer over coffee, a single verse, a song that lifts you up, or just taking a deep breath and inviting God into your morning before anyone else has your attention.

Here's what I know:

When you give God the first part of your day, no matter how small, no matter how messy, you invite something sacred into your life. You build a foundation that can't be shaken by challenges, chaos, or other people's moods. You remind yourself that you are covered, guided, and deeply loved.

So, if today feels heavy, or you're not sure where to start, try giving God just a moment. A word. A song. A thank you. You might be surprised how that small act can change the feel of your whole day.

Reflection: Put God First

What is the very first thing you reach for in the morning?

_____

_____

_____

_____

How do you want to feel as you step into your day?

_____

_____

_____

_____

If you could design your own morning ritual with God, no judgment, no pressure, what would it look like?

_____

_____

_____

_____

AFFIRMATION:

GOD GOES BEFORE ME. I AM COVERED, LOVED, AND READY TO BLOOM.

Chapter 2:
Watered by the Word (Feed Your Spirit)

Some seasons of life feel like survival. Maybe you know that place, a time when you are running on empty and even breathing feels like work. I remember being there. The days blurred together, the future was a big blank, and every moment seemed to demand more than I had to give. I learned then that a spirit left unfed becomes like dry, cracked soil where nothing healthy can grow.

Your spirit cannot thrive on whatever happens to fall into it. Just as a garden will not flourish on soda or saltwater, you cannot expect your spirit to flourish if you are constantly feeding it fear, gossip, or endless distraction. The soil of your soul needs the right kind of nourishment to grow strong and bear fruit.

Feeding your spirit means choosing what you allow in. For some, that might be reading a psalm before bed instead of scrolling through a phone. For others, it could be listening to a worship song during a lunch break or writing down a promise from God and placing it somewhere you will see it often. Scripture is living water. It seeps into the dry places, softens the hardened areas, and makes room for new roots to take hold.

Think of the verses you choose as seeds. Psalm 23 may plant comfort. Psalm 91 might plant protection. Isaiah 41:10 could plant courage. You do not have to plant them all at once, but plant something. Keep planting. And return to those seeds often, because even the healthiest garden needs tending.

The world will always try to plant weeds in your soil. But you decide which seeds stay and which ones get pulled. Feed your spirit truth. Feed it hope. Feed it words that build and not break.

Reflection: Feed Your Spirit

If your spirit is like soil, what has been planted there lately?

_____

_____

_____

Which "weeds" have you allowed to take root that you may need to pull out?

_____

_____

_____

What is one scripture, lyric, or prayer that waters your spirit every time you hear it?

_____

_____

_____

AFFIRMATION:

MY SPIRIT IS LIVING SOIL. I CHOOSE TO WATER IT WITH TRUTH, HOPE, AND THE WORD OF GOD SO THAT IT WILL GROW STRONG AND BEAR GOOD FRUIT.

Chapter 3:
Speak Life Over Your Garden
(Affirm Your Worth)

There was a time when I let every negative word spoken over me take root. Sometimes it wasn't even what others said, it was my own voice, whispering doubts and comparisons before my day even started. Maybe you know that voice, too. It can sound like, "You're not enough," or "Who do you think you are to want more?" That voice is a thief. It robs you of peace, joy, and potential.

Learning to affirm your worth isn't about ignoring reality or pretending everything is perfect. It's about choosing the seeds you want to plant in your own mind. The world will throw plenty of weeds your way, old stories, criticism, even well-meaning family who can't see your light. You get to decide what takes root.

But maybe you're not even sure *what* to affirm. Maybe you've never really sat with yourself and asked, "What do I want to believe about me?" Here's where you start:

» **Notice what you wish you heard growing up.** Did you long for someone to say, "I'm proud of you," or "You are enough"? Use that as your affirmation.

» **Pay attention to your struggles.** If you struggle with self-doubt, try "I am confident." If you're afraid to try, "I am brave." If you feel unseen, "I am valuable."

» **Write it in the present tense.** Not "I will be," but "I am." You're training your mind to recognize the truth now.

Don't be afraid to keep it simple:

"I am worthy."

"I am love."

"I am strong."

"I am allowed to take up space."

You can speak your affirmation out loud as you drive or play YouTube affirmations and let someone else's voice pour into your spirit. Place a sticky note on your bathroom mirror, like I did. Put one in your office, or on your dashboard. Let it be the thing you see, the soundtrack to your day, the reminder you need when you forget.

Plant these seeds daily. Every time a negative thought shows up, answer it with your affirmation. At first it may feel awkward, but that's okay. You're building a new habit, rewriting old patterns. Over time, you'll notice the weeds grow weaker, and the garden of your mind start to flourish.

Let yourself receive these truths. You are worthy. You are loved. You are already blooming, even if it's just a bud.

Reflection: Affirm Your Worth

What words did you need to hear growing up? How can you speak them over yourself now?

_____

_____

_____

Where in your daily routine can you see or hear affirmations?

_____

_____

_____

Write three new affirmations for the person you are becoming.

_____

_____

_____

AFFIRMATION:

I PLANT SEEDS OF TRUTH IN MY MIND EVERY DAY. I AM WORTHY,
AND I HONOR THAT WORTH WITH MY WORDS AND ACTIONS.

Chapter 4:
Keep Watch Over Your Garden
(Protect Your Energy)

This chapter is for the ones who love deeply, who want to be there for everyone, who grew up believing that being "good" means saying yes, even when it costs you everything.

Maybe you grew up in a house where boundaries didn't exist. Maybe you learned that love was giving until you were empty, or that it was your job to hold your family together, to be the fixer, the strong one, the always-available friend. Maybe you were taught that saying "no" is selfish, especially to family or people you've known your whole life.

But here's the truth, sometimes, the people closest to us are the ones who drain us most. It could be a parent, a sibling, a partner, or a childhood friend. You might love them, but every interaction leaves you feeling smaller, heavier, or more anxious. Sometimes it's the one who always needs to borrow, or the one who only calls to complain. Sometimes it's the family member who doesn't respect your choices, your boundaries, or your dreams.

This isn't easy to admit. Guilt can show up like an old friend, telling you you're wrong for needing space, for choosing yourself. But protecting your energy is *not* about cutting people off forever. It's about honoring your needs, setting boundaries, and allowing yourself to grow. You can love people and still limit their access. You can care and still say, "Not today." You can be kind and still say, "No."

What does this look like in real life?

> » *You stop answering every phone call, maybe let it go to voicemail and call back when you're ready.*

> » *You limit how much time you spend in draining conversations.*

> » *You change the subject when gossip or negativity starts or simply excuse yourself.*

> » *You create new traditions that nurture your spirit, even if it means disappointing someone else.*

> » *You recognize when your own energy is low, and you refill before you pour out again.*

If you're struggling with family, remember you didn't cause their pain, and you can't heal it by letting yourself be depleted. If it's old friends, remember seasons change, and not everyone is meant to go where you're going. If it's a partner, remember boundaries can bring you closer, because they let both people breathe.

Start with one small act of self-protection. Even if it feels awkward, even if someone pushes back, stand firm. Your energy is precious. The more you protect it, the more you'll have to give freely, joyfully and with an open heart.

You deserve to feel safe, supported, and whole.

Reflection: Protect Your Energy

Who in your life consistently drains your energy? How do you feel after spending time with them?

_____

_____

_____

What boundaries do you need to set, even if it feels uncomfortable?

_____

_____

_____

Where can you create space for your own healing and joy?

_____

_____

_____

AFFIRMATION:

MY ENERGY IS SACRED. I HAVE PERMISSION TO PROTECT MY PEACE, EVEN FROM THOSE I LOVE.

Chapter 5:
Prune with Purpose
(Control What You Can)

If you're someone who loves deeply, you've probably tried to fix or rescue people you care about. I know I have. I remember pouring my energy into trying to change someone I loved hoping my patience, kindness, or sacrifices would finally make them see their own potential. But the truth is, no matter how much love you give, you cannot force someone to grow, heal, or become who they are not yet ready to be.

There comes a point when the weight you've been carrying starts to feel heavier than your own life. When the tears, the prayers, and the bending over backwards still don't make a difference. That's when you learn: This isn't mine to fix.

You can't control how others treat you, what they believe about you, or the choices they make. You can control your response. You can control what you focus on, how you speak to yourself, and what you pour your energy into.

What happens when you shift your focus back to yourself? Suddenly, you notice all the things you *can* do, like take a class, learn a new skill, nurture a hobby, say yes to a new opportunity, or finally rest. That's not selfish, it's wise stewardship of the life God gave you.

Letting go doesn't mean you stop caring. It means you stop carrying what was never yours in the first place.

So today, ask yourself: Where am I spending my energy? On things I can change, or on things I cannot ? Can I redirect even a little bit of that energy toward my own growth, healing, and dreams?

You'll be amazed at what blooms when you start watering your own garden.

Reflection: Control What You Can

What have you tried to control that was never really yours to manage?

_____

_____

_____

Where in your life could you shift your focus inward?

_____

_____

_____

On a separate sheet of paper, write a release statement: "I let go of _____ so I can take care of myself."

_____

_____

_____

AFFIRMATION:

I LET GO OF WHAT I CANNOT CHANGE AND POUR MY ENERGY INTO WHAT HELPS ME GROW.

Chapter 6:
Let Curiosity Blossom
(Ask Questions Without Fear)

For years, I used to think asking questions made me look weak. So, I kept my thoughts to myself, nodded along, and hoped no one would notice the things I didn't know. And when I did speak up, the people I trusted most sometimes laughed, rolled their eyes, or made me feel small for not already knowing. It taught me to stay quiet, even when I wanted to understand

It wasn't until a wise manager pulled me aside and said, "If you don't ask, how will you ever learn?" that I realized how wrong I'd been. She gave me permission to be curious, to admit what I didn't know, to seek wisdom. That single lesson changed everything.

Here's the secret: Life is a classroom, not a test you have to pass without help. Growth begins when you give yourself permission to wonder, to dig deeper, and to speak up, especially when you feel unsure. The bravest people are often the ones who are willing to say, "I don't know, but I want to learn."

Asking questions isn't just about getting answers; it's about opening doors. It's about honoring your desire to grow. It's how you learn, how you connect, how you create opportunities.

Is there something you've been afraid to ask at work, in your relationships, in your faith? Where have you held your tongue, hoping nobody would notice your uncertainty? Imagine what might change if you let yourself be a beginner again.

Remember: every expert was once a beginner; every wise woman once asked her first question. There is power in your curiosity. Give yourself permission to use it.

Reflection: Ask Questions Without Fear

What's one question you've been afraid to ask? What's the story behind that fear?

_____

_____

_____

Where in your life could you use more curiosity instead of judgment?

_____

_____

_____

Write a question you want to ask this week, at work, at home, or with God. Then ask it.

_____

_____

_____

AFFIRMATION:

MY QUESTIONS ARE A GIFT. I AM BRAVE ENOUGH TO SEEK, TO LEARN, AND TO GROW.

Chapter 7:
Choose Your Gardener Wisely
(Choose Your Circle Wisely)

If you want to know the secret to a healthy, vibrant garden, look at the hands that tend it.

Who is watering your roots? Who is planting seeds of possibility in your spirit?

The people you allow close are your gardeners. Some will help you bloom. Some will only pull the petals off your dreams.

There's a moment I will never forget.

After years of separation, my father and I reconnected. He'd moved to New Orleans, and we were sitting quietly in his living room, catching up on the missing years. I started telling him about my husband's accomplishments, all the ways he had succeeded, the things he had done for our family, I thought I was simply catching him up. He listened, then paused, looked at me with care and gentleness, and asked:

"But what about you?"

Those four words landed in my spirit like sunlight.

That's what a true gardener does, sees the soil and invites life to take root. My father's question planted a seed in me: "Who is nurturing *you*?"

It made me realize how rare, how precious, it is to have someone who truly wants to see you bloom, not for their benefit, but for your own.

When you're building your life, be mindful of the gardeners you choose.

Some people will pour water on your dreams, cheer for your growth, and protect your roots when the winds come. Others, sometimes even family, might see your past or point out your flaws, but never offer the support you need to grow.

Who in your life...

» Celebrates when you bloom?

» Reminds you to reach for the sun, even when you feel small?

» Protects your peace, even when you forget how?

» Plants seeds of encouragement, hope, faith, and truth in your soil?

And who pulls at your petals, drains your energy, or shades you from the sunlight you need?

It's okay to move certain people to the outer edges of your garden.

It's okay to close the gate.

It's okay to outgrow those who cannot or will not help you thrive.

You can still love them, pray for them, and wish them well. But you do not have to let everyone tend your soil.

Instead, look for gardeners, mentors, friends, elders, even strangers who pour wisdom and sunlight into you.

The ones who *see* you, water you, and remind you: you were made to bloom, not just survive.

And don't forget: **be a gardener for others, too**. The best gardens are built by hands that both give and receive.

Reflection: Choose Your Gardener Wisely

Who are the gardeners in your life, the people who nourish your spirit, water your dreams, and encourage your growth?

_____

_____

Who might need to be moved to the edges of your garden so your roots can strengthen?

_____

_____

What qualities do you want in the gardeners who tend your soul?

_____

_____

How can you become a gardener for someone else today?

_____

_____

AFFIRMATION:

I CHOOSE GARDENERS WHO NOURISH MY SOUL, WATER MY
DREAMS, AND CELEBRATE MY BLOOMING.

Chapter 8:
Weather the Storms
(You Can Do Hard Things)

There was a time when the phrase *"I can do hard things"* felt too big for me. I remember staring at my college books, my to-do list, and the weight of everything happening in my personal life, thinking, *"This is too much."* But every time I showed up, even when I was tired, afraid, or doubting myself, I discovered a little more strength than I had the day before.

Hard things are rarely comfortable. They stretch you, test you, and sometimes make you question whether you have what it takes. But here's the thing: you've already survived things you once thought you couldn't. Think about that. You've already climbed mountains you once thought were impossible.

When you start telling yourself, *"I can do hard things,"* you plant a seed in your mind. At first, it might feel small, almost fragile. But the more you speak it, the deeper it roots. Over time, that seed grows into courage, discipline, and resilience. And when the next challenge comes, that mindset is already there, ready to help you climb again.

Tips for living out "I can do hard things":

» Write the phrase somewhere you'll see it every day — mirror, phone screen, car dashboard.

» Break your challenge into smaller steps so you can track progress without feeling overwhelmed.

» Keep reminders of past victories — photos, notes, or a "victory journal" you can read on hard days.

» Surround yourself with voices that believe in you, especially when yours feels shaky.

» Treat rest as part of the work — you can do hard things and still take care of your body and mind.

Every challenge you face is a chance to prove to yourself that you're stronger than you thought. You don't have to do it perfectly. You just have to keep showing up.

Reflection: You Can Do Hard Things

What is one hard thing you've already accomplished or survived?

_____

_____

What challenge are you facing right now that needs your courage?

_____

_____

How will you remind yourself of your strength when you start to doubt?

_____

_____

AFFIRMATION:

"I AM RESILIENT. I CAN DO HARD THINGS, AND I GROW STRONGER WITH EVERY STEP."

Chapter 9:
Pull the Weeds, Plant the Truth
(Block Out Negativity)

Negativity can come from anywhere, a co-worker, a family member, social media, or even the little voice in your head that whispers you're not enough. I've learned that you can't always control when negativity shows up, but you *can* control whether it gets to stay.

Remember that your mind is your garden. The things you dwell on are the seeds you plant. Negativity is like weeds; it will grow quickly if you give it room. Positivity, gratitude, and faith are like flowers. They require your attention, your protection, and your intentional watering.

For me, blocking out negativity means being selective about who and what I give my time to. It might mean taking a social media break, asking to return to a hard topic so I can give myself time to breathe, putting on gospel music to shift the atmosphere, or going for a walk to clear my mind. Sometimes it's as simple as replacing a negative thought with an affirmation I've already planted.

Ways to block out negativity:

» Limit your exposure to people, places, or media that drain you.

» Keep uplifting music, affirmations, or scripture close for a quick mindset reset.

» Practice saying, *"That's your opinion; I believe otherwise."*

» Redirect gossip into gratitude - talk about what's good instead of what's wrong.

» Surround yourself with people who pour light into you, not darkness.

Remember: what you water will grow. If you feed the negative thoughts, they will multiply. If you feed the positive ones, they will flourish. Choose wisely.

Reflection: Block Out Negativity

Where is negativity showing up most in your life right now?

_____

_____

_____

What's one thing you can do this week to limit its influence?

_____

_____

_____

What positive truth can you speak over yourself when negativity appears?

_____

_____

_____

AFFIRMATION:

"I CHOOSE PEACE. I CHOOSE JOY. I CHOOSE TO WATER ONLY
WHAT I WANT TO GROW."

Chapter 10:
Savor Every Bloom
(Celebrate Small Wins)

Sometimes it feels like the world only claps for the big victories, the graduation, the promotion, the house, the wedding. But if you've ever been in a season of rebuilding, heartbreak, or healing, you know that the *real* miracles are often quiet.

They're found in the moments when you show up for yourself, even when no one is watching.

They're in the tiny acts of courage, the days you choose hope instead of hiding, or the simple decision to keep going when you wanted to quit.

Maybe your "win" today is getting out of bed when anxiety tries to keep you under the covers.

Maybe it's drinking water, making a phone call, sending a prayer, or saying "no" to something that used to drain you.

Maybe it's forgiving yourself for something old, or choosing to rest without guilt.

Small wins are the heartbeat of transformation. They're the way you remind yourself, day by day, that you're still moving, still growing, still alive.

For a long time, I looked for someone else to notice my efforts, to applaud my progress. Sometimes people clapped; sometimes they were too wrapped up in their own lives to see me at all. That used to sting. But I learned that waiting for validation from others will keep you starving for affirmation you can give yourself.

What if you became your own biggest cheerleader?

What if you decided that every step, no matter how tiny, deserves acknowledgment?

What if you stopped measuring yourself by someone else's milestones and started honoring your own rhythm?

Celebrate when you choose yourself.

Celebrate when you set a boundary.

Celebrate when you finally rest, after years of hustling without pause.

Celebrate when you learn to forgive, to let go, or to trust again.

Buy yourself flowers. Write yourself a note. Take yourself out on a date. Do a victory dance in the kitchen.

Or just sit quietly and thank God that you made it through another hard day.

There will always be people who won't understand the size of your win because they didn't walk your road. That's okay. Your healing is sacred, and so are your victories, no matter how small.

Remember: flowers don't bloom all at once.

Growth happens in slow, steady bursts, sometimes unseen, but always miraculous.

Every step forward matters, even if you're the only one who notices.

This is your permission to celebrate.

Your journey is worthy of joy.

Your small wins are building a bigger, brighter future, one gentle step at a time.

Reflection: Celebrate Small Wins

Name one thing you did this week, big or small that makes you proud. Write it down and let yourself feel it.

_____

_____

_____

How do you usually acknowledge your progress? How could you start making this a regular practice?

_____

_____

_____

If you struggle to celebrate yourself, ask: Where did that belief come from, and how can you rewrite it?

_____

_____

_____

AFFIRMATION:

EVERY WIN, NO MATTER THE SIZE, MATTERS. I HONOR MY PROGRESS, CELEBRATE MY JOURNEY, AND WATER MY SPIRIT WITH GRATITUDE.

You Did It! You Bloomed

Look at you. Really take a minute and see what you've done here.

You made it to the end of this workbook. You kept showing up, page after page, even when life tried to crowd out your sunlight.

Maybe you wrote your first affirmation, or maybe you found the courage to set a boundary. Maybe you just read and reflected and let the truth settle into your spirit.

No matter how you moved through these pages, you did it. You chose to water your own soul. You chose growth, even when it wasn't easy.

Are you blooming? I hope so.

Is your soul a little more nourished than before? I pray it is.

But listen, if you need to, come back. Flip through these chapters as many times as you want. Life changes. You change. Some lessons won't make sense today, but next season, they'll bloom in you.

This is your journey. Take all the time you need. And know that I'm rooting for you, every step of the way.

There's nothing I'd love more than to hear your story. Seriously, email me, message me on Instagram, let me know what changed for you. Your story matters. Your healing matters.

We're all out here, growing in our own way. Let's celebrate together!

If you want more encouragement or just want to share your progress, connect with me on Instagram @bloomandsipguide or email me at bloomandsipguide@gmail.com.
I can't wait to see your "bloom" moments!

And remember: your growth is sacred. Your wins, your stumbles, your rest days, they all count. Keep blooming, one gentle step at a time.

Scripture for the Road

> "THE RIGHTEOUS WILL FLOURISH LIKE A PALM TREE, THEY WILL GROW LIKE A CEDAR OF LEBANON; PLANTED IN THE HOUSE OF THE LORD, THEY WILL FLOURISH IN THE COURTS OF OUR GOD."
>
> —PSALM 92:12–13 [NIV]

With all my love and hope,

Sorena

About the Author

Sorena Washington-Briley is a creative entrepreneur and faith inspired writer from New Orleans, Louisiana. She is passionate about encouraging others to grow through life's seasons and blends personal insight with practical tools to help women nurture their spirit and embrace their full potential. As a photographer and artist, Sorena has a natural eye for beauty in both images and everyday moments that tell a story. Her creative approach flows into her writing, making her work both relatable and deeply inspiring. When she is not creating, Sorena enjoys jogging, listening to gospel music, and spending quality time with her family. Bloom & Sip is her invitation for readers to slow down, pour into themselves, and watch their own growth take root.

www.ingramcontent.com/pod-product-compliance
Lightning Source LLC
Chambersburg PA
CBHW041526120626
46551CB00018B/2588